A Peace of Our Minds

Compiled by :
Shona McCarthy
Adele Plant
Ann Marie Pettit
Aoife O'Connor
Ruth Bailey

Foreword by
Brendan Kennelly

Edited by:
Carol McGrath

Design and Layout by:
Tony Hetherington

GW00802411

This Edition first published 1996 by

Mentor Press

43 Furze Road,
Sandyford Industrial Estate,
Dublin 18.

Tel. (01) 295 2112/3   Fax. (01) 295 2114

This collection of poems Copyright © 1996
Mentor Press with Wesley College

Foreword Copyright © 1996 Brendan Kennelly

Poems Copyright © 1996 the individual contributors

ISBN : 0 947548 95 5

1 3 5 7 9 10 8 6 4 2

Cover Illustration: Don Conroy

Printed in Ireland by ColourBooks

2

Contents

4

FOREWORD

I found it difficult to arrive at a final judgment of these poems because several of them seemed to me to be worthy of a prize. In fact, if I had my way I'd have given a prize to all the poems I was privileged to read; they all had something interesting to say and they usually said it in a clear, convincing way.

The poems show that these students have thought deeply about peace, and therefore about war, violence, tensions, all the dark forces that are always waiting to disrupt peace. Peace is a threatened beauty; and we must struggle to preserve it.

I think it's wonderful that people of relatively few years have such important things to say about peace in these poems. The world could learn from them.

The winning poems are Christopher Middleton's *I Hardly Know* and Cara Quinn Larkin's *A White Flower.* I've read these poems many times. They're memorable.
I'll finish with two lines from Kevin Hawkins' poem:

> *Peace is like a summer's day in winter,*
> *War is like thunder on a summer's day.*

Is it any wonder I'd like to give a prize to every writer in this collection?

September 1996

Brendan Kennelly.

Preface

A Peace of Our Minds began as a project, in early 1996, when the Peace Process, scarcely eighteen months old, was suddenly disrupted by the Canary Wharf bombing. I and a group of Fifth Year students from Wesley College, wanted to give young people the opportunity to express their hopes and aspirations for a peaceful resolution to the 'Troubles' in our country.

We wrote to all the primary and second-level schools in Belfast and Dublin, inviting students to submit poems on the theme of 'Peace'. The response was tremendous. Many of the poems submitted were very moving and quite impressive. Written by children from the ages of 4 to 17 years, the poems exemplify the idealism, innocence and unique perceptiveness often displayed by young children and teenagers.

Sadly, the poems also reflect the personal suffering directly experienced by some of the children who submitted poems.

We hope you enjoy this memorable collection of poems. It shows that young people have very strong views on 'Peace' and 'Conflict'.

The royalties from this book will be donated to UNICEF (the Children's Fund). By buying this book you are supporting a good cause and recognising the importance of what peace means to young people.

The 'voices' of the 'young poets' in this collection, may, perhaps, just contribute to the general will and resolve for peace in our country.

The publication of this book was possible due to the generosity and contribution of many people.

I would like to thank:-

Adele Plant
Ann-Marie Pettit
Aoife O'Connor
Ruth Bailey . . . for all their help and support;

Mr Derek Shaw for his guidance and encouragement
Professor Brendan Kennelly who kindly selected the prize-winning poems;
Ms Sandra Cooke and Ms Ida Reed who both had the unenviable task of shortlisting for publication, a number of the many poems submitted.
The Principal and Board of Governors of Wesley College for facilitating and supporting the project.

I would especially like to thank the hundreds of children who sent us their poems. In particular, I wish to acknowledge the enthusiastic response from the children and young adults of Belfast. I realise that the influences and problems of the 'Troubles' have never been far from their young lives.

Shona McCarthy
Wesley College
October 1996

Royalties from this book go to

A White Flower

A child with a snow white flower
in front of the charging war.

A child with a snow white flower,
never seen there before.

A child with a snow white flower,
dressed in white just like a dove.

A child with a snow white flower,
as if sent from God above.

A child with a snow white flower,
death lingering all around.

A child with a snow white flower
not hearing the deafening sound.

A child with a snow white flower,
hoping the war is gone.

A child with a snow white flower,
so that revolution may come.

Cara Quinn Larkin
Age 10

St Brigid's National School
Glasnevin
Dublin

I Hardly Know

I hardly know why you chose to pour me out your heart
But we have our hates in common, and that's at least a start.
Your trouble is you take it in, you listen to them all,
And I'm your paper soldier, behind a concrete wall.
You know just what I'm after, you've seen it come for miles,
But I like you 'cause you humour me with million dollar smiles
And eyes that seem to hoover up all surrounding light
And talk about a future that stretches past tonight.

The words pour down like stair-rods, I never stop to think,
In my vanity I cannot see the glass from which you drink.
Perhaps I haven't listened to a single word you said,
Through rose-tint glass you cannot see the signals turn to red,
And every time I make a move, you break into a run,
You're scared in case you're poisoned by my silver tongue.
You rake up former lovers and I can't work out why
(Now I see, before "we" were born, that "we " began to die).

Poetic justice says that you get just desserts from life,
My paper lies could be dissected by a paper knife.
I'm slow upon the uptake, I'm buried in the sand,
All that I have left of you is scrawled upon my hand
And all we said evaporates, at the break of day,
I've got my bravado back, and you your normal ways.
But sometimes, when I catch your glimpse across a crowded street
I tell myself I'm dreaming when my heart has missed a beat.

Christopher Middleton
Age 16

Methodist College
Belfast

Belfast Peace

*B*elfast has been split for so many years,
  *E*nveloped in an array of bitter tears,
    *L*aughter lost when killings begin,
      *F*ew people know of the pain within.
        A city divided, will we ever stand?
          *S*ought after friendship, the shake of a hand,
            *T*ime will tell but we can't fix the past.

*P*eace talks and meetings we hope will last,
  *E*nvy and hatred overwhelm us all,
    *A*cceptance and tolerance, the new writing on the wall,
      *C*atholics and Protestants never as one?
        *E*ager to believe that the time will soon come.

Claire Rattican
Age 13

St Genevieve's High School
Belfast

Silver Stars

Peace means to me
the quiet countryside.
And the quiet night of
a bright moon and
silver stars of peace.

Peace means to me
no bombs, no shooting
and no wars. Just a
playful sunny day.

Peace means to me
a peaceful world.
No killings, no bad
things, just a
peaceful world.

Peace is a calm sea
with a marvellous key -
To a door of peace
on the other side.

hon

ional School

The Spirit Of My Country

Earth and water don't bind my country,
Her spirit unwinds on a mystic breeze.
Uncorrupted by credence or currency,
Her anthem elusive, twists through the trees.
Hazard and haste don't blind my country,
Time cannot waste her immortal charm.
Shyly seductive, she induces an empathy,
A haven from hatred, a shelter from harm.
She hums with an energy, magnetic but soft,
Enticing the fearful, like magpies to gold.
Absorbing the tearful laments of the lost,
Restoring a yearning for futures untold.

My country remains obscure and uncharted,
But she draws me to her when hope has departed.

Katya Mealy
Age 17

The King's Hospital
Palmerstown
Dublin

15

Peace, Peace, Peace.

Peace, peace, peace.
Love, love, love.
These are the stoppers of war!
The flash of the gun,
From which people run,
Shall be banished,
Once and for all!
The noise of the bomb,
From which families are gone,
Shall be quietened once and for all!

Huw Duffy
1st Class,

School unknown.

Open Eyes

There once was a time when I had realized
That all I had to do was open my eyes,
Then talk to this enemy I had despised.
Then came the time to open the door,
To walk outside and be totally sure.
I went to the enemy I had despised
And realized he had opened his eyes.
We met on the street with dirt on our feet,
I looked at him, he looked at me,
Then we could see with no disguise.

Both of us had opened our eyes.

David Graver
Age 11

Scoil Chrónáin
Rathcoole
Co. Dublin

The Terrorist

As a child, he was told who to play with,
How to feel when killings reached the news.
His parents kept him from "those people",
As was safest, in their view.

As a child he was innocent, seeing all as friends,
But fed on a diet of half-truths and lies,
He hated "them" for past generations' sins.
The hate within him grew until the innocence died.

Those he respected formed his mind,
As he learned the half-truths and lies,
Warped by the passage of time,
Telling how "they" lived their lives.

Moulded by hatred, he learned to fight,
Killing "them" before they killed him.
He killed randomly, they were all the same
In his view, they all lived lives of sin

For the iniquity of their forefathers.
Caught in the cycle of a terrorist group
That coerced him to kill more,
That thought dead children a coup.

Twisted lies and hatred got him killed
By an assassin, one of "them",
A murderer, cold-blooded and ruthless,
Who had grown up just like him.

Geoff Lillis
Age 15

Scoil Chaitríona
Glasnevin
Dublin

All Party Peace Talks

Three men, fat like footballs, waddle into a pub,
Curry rolling around in their stomachs.
They buy pints and sit down.
"Jesus it's awful, the bombing and that,"
"Yeah, I'm sick of this violence lark,"
"Indeed, something has to be sorted out,"
"So, who fancies Liverpool for the premiership?"

Mark Hanrahan
Age 18

Sutton Park School
Dublin

Opening Doors

After twenty-five years of unstoppable war
People have learned to open their doors.
Their worries and fears all now have stopped
And they can now sleep in their beds
Like babies in a cot.

Before the ceasefire we lived in fear,
Knowing there might be a gunman near.
We watched the parades as the people sang,
Keeping our ears peeled for the slightest BANG!

We laughed, we cried, we shared our fears,
But all the time we were holding back our tears.

Some daughters, some husbands and some sons,
All got killed by people with guns.

We all live in hope that one day
All our dreams will come our way.
We want all the shooting and bombing to stop
So then our babies can sleep well in their cots.

Judith Mc Knight
Age 10

St Luke's Primary School
Twinbrook
Belfast

What Peace And War Are To Me

When I think of peace it is silent and quiet,
I think war is noisy and violent.

Peace means not avoiding a group of teenagers,
War makes you look out the window before going out.

Peace is like a summer's day in winter,
War is like thunder on a summer's day.

Kevin Hawkins
Age 11

St Teresa's Primary School
Glen Road
Belfast

War And Peace

Each night we look
down on you.
Our eyes glazed in
terror and anger.

You cannot see us
but we are there
watching.

When at night you lie
sleepless, guilty and afraid,
we gaze upon you.
Your fatal bullets
still in our flesh.

We come in all shapes
and sizes.
Young, old, men, women,
so many innocent.

We look down on you
and pity you.
You have quenched
our lives,
but our hope for peace
still burns.

Our ghostly tears fall
softly on a place
where the dove
has become a bird
of prey.

Aoife Doyle
Age 14
Sutton Park School
Dublin

Pray For Peace

"Fenian, Taig" is all that I hear,
While I sit on the bus stiff with fear,
My heart is pounding as fast as can be.
They know that I'm nervous because they grin with glee.
I look out of the window pretending to be occupied,
But my mind triggers back to all the people that have died.
I think of all the innocent and defenceless people that have
lost their lives,
Of all the people that have grieved for their husbands
and wives.
I'm distracted by somebody pulling my hair.
I want to look round but I do not dare.
I feel tears swelling in my eyes.
"Leave him alone," I hear somebody cry,
"It doesn't matter what religion we are.
We're all just the same, so stop playing this foolish game.
Maybe you think you're tough.
Maybe you think you're rough.
Stop acting "cool" because it's just pointless and cruel."
I looked around at the other boy that had spoken, tall
and well-built.
Then I looked at the other boy who was red with guilt.
When I got home I cried, not for me, but for our divisions,
For all the people that have died and for all the relatives
that had gone through so much pain and agony.
I hope that we have the strength to pray for peace
despite our differences.

Patrick Maxwell
Age 14

St Patrick's Secondary School
Antrim Road
Belfast

Canary Wharf

canary: cage songbird of yellow plumage
wharf: platform to where ships may be moored to
         load and unload

A bird so used to bars
They have become a way of life.
Caged yellow plumage
That wept that solemn night.

And ships and ships of politicians
Unloaded in the docks,
"Of course we worked for peace, ma'am,
Now tick my little box."

"Please, surely it was more than this,
More than a voting game,"
Wails re-caged yellow-feathered hope,
Her lock grinds shut again.

Onto the dusty ghost-town wharf,
New-same grey suits appear,
Chirping condemning, condoning words.
Hope sheds a bitter tear.

Ruth O'Byrnes
Age 16

Sutton Park School
Dublin

24

Peace is . . .

Peace is living in harmony,
happily with your family.

Peace is no killings
or bombings in towns.

Peace is happiness
all around.

Peace is no policemen
watching the streets.

Peace is no robberies
or fear of being shot.

Peace is putting guns down,
forever locked away.

Peace is everything that
everyone wants in Belfast.

Patrick Forte
Age 9

St Luke's Primary School
Twinbrook
Belfast

War

I stood as a child on top of the mountain
The sky hung like a veil of blinding light
For a split second, then it was gone
And I heard the shot ringing out in the distance.
My innocence was no more.

I saw and felt and smelt the blackness,
the hate, the violence that hangs like a black cloud over us all,
shrouding us.
I heard the cries of pain and fear as death hovered,
silently, and overcame its victim.
But when the clouds had cleared I saw the dove and knew
there was still HOPE.

Emily Byrne
Age 13

Coláiste Íosagáin
Stillorgan
Dublin

'Happily Ever After'

A barbarous sieve of forgotten nothings drains efficient recollections,
Silent smirks echo ghostly paradigms of smothering torches,
A gloved digit recoils with serpentine judgement
And darkness.

David Sheane
Age 17

Sutton Park School
Dublin

Twelfth Of July

A story my Mum once told me:
On the twelfth of July each year,
Where bands would play and sing about
The "Battle of the Boyne",
After the parade the men would roam
For a place to put down their drums.
My Grandma had a big soft heart
And allowed them leave them in her hall,
But it didn't seem strange to any of them then,
Even though my grandma was a 'papist'
And they were 'orange' men.

Hannah Scott
Age 12

Scoil Mhuire
Sandymount
Dublin

Peace

I would want some peace in Ireland.
I would like no bombs and shooting.
I would not like people to get shot
And no bombs through the letterbox.
I would not like men bombing houses
And stealing things out of people's houses.

Jade Armstrong
Age 7

(School unknown)
Belfast

The Red Hand And Shamrock Sprigs

I switch the T.V. on
but there's nothing to watch,
nothing feels comforting as the anxiety thickens,
where have my parents gone?

Walking to the kitchen,
the T.V. still heard,
I want to see my dad in here again.
No, I will look, I'm being absurd.

It says ten past four on the red hand of the clock
beside the plastic sprigs of shamrock in a vase.
Both have been there for years beside each other,
even before I was born,
and both have given no compliment to the kitchen,
picking up dust and fading away, forlorn.

My parents are just an hour late,
and they said they might be delayed,
but then why did Aunt May 'phone to ask
if they were back yet? I mean,
the Falls Road isn't that far away!

From the kitchen I hear the newsreader,
her solemn voice becomes clear,
and running to the T.V. set
I stub my toe due to nervousness and fear.

"A car bomb has gone off on the Falls Road,
casualties are unknown as yet," she speaks
and I hear screaming in my head.
My question has been answered,
my parents are really dead.

My legs give in and my head hits my knees,
and from the garden my dog begins to bark.
The excitedness of the sound registers in my mind,
so I open my eyes and feel safe from the dark.

The second sound is the key in the door,
which leads into the third,
"We're home pet, sorry we're late, we
found that the car doesn't take unleaded anymore".

Debbie Bonnar
Age 14

Methodist College,
Belfast

Ireland, I Can Hear You Cry

You live on an island that changed from peace to war,
What have we gained?
I have fields of green and valleys of gold,
Now my legends shall not be told.

Ireland, I can see and hear
You cry, because peace was once so near,
With killing and bombs, heartache and pain.
Dear God, give her back peace again.

Why did it happen, can anyone explain
Twenty-five years of hatred and pain?
Why did it happen, can anyone explain
Why do I hold my head in shame?

Jackie Maguire
Age 15

St Genevieve's High School
Belfast

Peace and War

Leaves rustling remind me of peace.
Guns and bombs remind me of war.
Listening to dogs barking, cats miaowing is peaceful.
Blood running, bombs going isn't peaceful.
White is for peace.
Red is for war.

The End.

Freda Ní Dhomhnaill
Age 6

Scoil Bhríde
Ranelagh
Dublin

What Did She Do?

What did she do
To anger those men,
Who murdered her parents
When she was just ten?
Nothing. War means nothing.

What can she see?
Just bullets and guns,
Bombs and bruises,
Dead daughters, dead sons.
Nothing. War means nothing.

What can we do
To see peace in our time?
We can stop all this fighting,
Murder and crime.
Everything. Peace is everything.

Lindsay Murphy
Age 10

Howth Road National School
Clontarf
Dublin

Divisions/Deighilt

The boy lay sobbing on the bed,
life had no meaning, his father was dead.
A better Dad would be hard to find,
but the people who killed him didn't seem to mind.
He was a peace loving Protestant, maybe that's why,
but that's no reason for a man to die.

Chuala sí an doras ag dúnadh go ciúin.
Téann a Daidí amach gach Luan.
Níl a fhios aici cá bhfuil sé ag dul.
Tá sí ina haonar, tosnaíonn sí ag gol.
Níl aon gaolta eile fágtha aici.
Thóg buama mór a máthair uaithi.

A weeping wife lies alone in her bed,
memories of him linger strong in her head.
All that's left for her are shattered dreams,
her wonderful life falls apart at the seams.
Two children left to raise all alone,
her unborn baby leaps for a father unknown.

Ar a trí a chlog chuala sí torann sa halla.
Bhí a Daidí ar ais, bhí sé ag cur fola.
Bhí na poilíní ag teacht ar a thóir,
is iad a fhocail deireadh ná "Slán a stóir!"
Ball don IRA is ea a h-athair, chuaigh sé go gaol.
An iníon agus an athair, scartha go deireadh a saoil.

We see lives torn apart in the North by the war.
We all want peace, fighting no more.
Whether English or Irish, together let's shout:
"Tá an tsíocháin uainn - cinnte gan dabht!"

Caitríona Ní Dhuibhne, Age 16,
and Emer Ní Ríain, Age 16

Scoil Mhuire
Templeogue
Dublin

Peace not Pieces

I love to go out and run.
To tumble around in fun.
To feel i can go far and near.
With never a fright or fear.
But oh its bad so very bad.
And thats what makes it all so sad.
Instead of fun and the bright sun.
We have the darkness of the gun.

Ann-Marie McDonagh age 10

Or else while we jump and play.
We may all be blown away.
While running down an incline.
We are caught by a land mine.

Martin Lynch age 10

I am a traveller boy.
I would like to live in joy.
So please let all wars cease.
That we may be in peace.

The following poem was written and illustrated by children from the Travelling Community, who attend St Columba's School and Day Care Centre in Dublin.

Peace Not Pieces

I love to go out and run,
To tumble around in fun,
To feel I can go far and near,
With never a fright or fear.

But oh, it's bad, so very bad,
And that's what makes it all so sad.
Instead of fun and the bright sun
We have the darkness of the gun.

I am a traveller boy.
I would like to live in joy.
So please let all wars cease,
That we may be in peace.

Or else, while we jump and play,
We may all be blown away.
While running down an incline,
We are caught by a landmine.

Poem by: Martin Lynch
Age 10
Illustrations by: Ann-Marie McDonagh
Age 10

St Columba's School
Great Strand St.
Dublin

When You Think Of The Troubles

When you think of the troubles, you think of pain,
You think of the crying people and the loved ones they have
lost.
You think of what is going on
And you want it all to stop.

When you think of the troubles, you think of
Soldiers, you think of terrorists,
You think of bombs and you think of guns,
And you think of the destruction that has been caused.

When you think of the troubles, you think of
Catholics and Protestants,
You think of Jews and Germans,
You think of politics, party talks, greed and patrols.
But you want to think of peace.

When I think of the troubles, I think of these words,
I
Want
Peace.

Glen Dower
Age 12

(School unknown)
Belfast

Peace Is Love

Peace is Love.
Peace is Joy.
Peace is Silence and Quiet.
Peace means
No more fighting and
No more killing.

Deborah Doherty
Age 6

Mother of Divine Grace Infant School
Dublin

It Starts With You

They glared at each other from across the street,

Each man sticking to his own side,

Not daring to make a closer move

Or to back away,

No, for that would be cowardly,

In their eyes that just wouldn't do.

The staring went on for what seemed like hours,

Nothing, just quiet, stillness all around,

And then . . . slowly

Up stepped the two leaders,

"We come to make peace," said one Catholic boy,

"Go to hell," said the Protestant in reply,

"We'd never stoop to that low, low depth

As to make peace with the people we hate."

So there they stood, quiet, without a word.

Then suddenly, from the back of the Protestant crowd,

A boy threw a hateful brick.

It sailed high over the rest of the crowd

And hit a Catholic in the eye,

That 's when the fighting started.

Abuse was hurled between the two sides

And, alas, that wasn't all that was hurled.

Yet they are so young!

Who teaches them this hatred,

The hatred they have for each other?

I'll tell you who,

It's the older generation.

We see the news and think it's right to fight,

No one tells us different

Because they themselves are too busy fighting.

But if all this fighting were to stop,

And the hatred died away,

We'd learn to love our other side,

Not hate them in every way.

The children would stop and turn and think,

Realise the fighting has got to stop,

They turn back and smile a smile,

Shake hands and make a truce.

So, it starts with you, responsible adults,

Who claim you know it all,

You've got to try and make the peace,

If not for your sakes, then please, for ours.

Eleanor Baroise
Age 13

Newpark Comprehensive School
Blackrock,
Co.Dublin

Peace And War In Our Country

Let us have peace in our country.
Let us have love in our land.
Why can't we all live together?
Why can't they all understand
That love and peace in our country
Will let children walk hand-in-hand?

Why can't we all stand together?
Why can't we all shout as one,
"War is bad,
War is sad,
Let peace come to Ireland".

Aisling Leavey
Age 9

Star of the Sea Primary School
Belfast

This poem was written by a class of 4 and 5 year olds after observing a minute's silence for peace. Each line was written by a different child.

Peace

Peace is quiet.

It's riding on a boat.

It's when no one's shouting or crying.

Peace is when you're sleeping.

Peace means relaxing.

Peace is to stop crying.

Peace is riding on an aeroplane.

It's going for a walk.

It's resting.

It's listening to music.

It's riding on a pony.

Peace means when they don't want any wars.

They don't want anyone to fight in their country.

When you're on your own you're in peace.

The Infants of
Sutton Park School
Dublin

Memories

Living in Ireland can be so wonderful,
Watching kids play on street roads,
But the memories of my life in Belfast
Aren't as good as some of those.

The person I loved and was so close to
Is no longer living, she was killed.
For the days that I cried
In grief and sorrow,
The anger that I kept inside,
For which I longed to let out,
I will tomorrow.

The nights that I spend
Wondering what life could be like
In peace and not war,
In light and not darkness.

It's funny that in Belfast
You can't go out anymore,
That Catholics and Protestants
Play their merry war.

If only they would realise
What they are doing to us.
We don't want a childhood
Full of hatred and war.
We want a childhood
Full of love and care,
Of peace and happiness,
That our children might share.

Claire O'Connor
Age 13

St Genevieve's High School
Belfast

Síocháin

Síocháin. Cad í?

Daoine gan eagla faoi
Spéir álainn an Earraigh.
Ag dul anseo is ansiúd
Lena chéile gan namhaid?

Saol gan pléascanna móra
Faoin gcarr sa siopa.
Saol gan teaghlach briste?

Agus rudaí mar sin?
An bhfuil sibh ag éisteacht?
B'fhéidir go mbeadh síocháin
I bhur meabhracha freisin
Dá n-éistfeadh sibh.

Alastair Matthews
Age 16

Wesley College
Dublin

45

Nothing To Gain

Look at the paper and what do you see?
Headlines of shootings, bombings and death,
Pain, anger, hurt, sorrow and threat.
Why is it so that this has to be?.
What is the point, that's what I can't see.
When will it end, when will we be free -
Free of the worry, the fear and the pain,
This life of war from which we've nothing to gain?

So many lives lost, so many tears shed,
So many angry words spoken, so many people dead.
Imagine to die because of wrong place or wrong time,
To be an innocent victim of a heartless crime.
In those six counties, in every pair of eyes,
You will see the fear and the hatred, the shock and the pain,
The questions asking why, what have we to gain?

Will it ever end? Will it ever stop?
Will there ever be a night where we can sleep in peace,
No fear of bombs, of relatives being shot,
Of children being kidnapped, of lives being lost?
Dear God, please let us be,
Give us the peace
And it will set us free.

Stacey Cahill
Age 14

Pobalscoil Neasáin
Baldoyle
Dublin

On War And Peace

He sees fresh blood diffuse upon white cloth
But is not moved to pity or remorse.
He surely will bow 'neath his own God's wrath ,
For 'neath a just God's standard rears his horse.
Hypocrisy - the scourge of humankind.
Affected smiles and lies which mask the hate,
But any fool can see what lies behind
The callous murderer, so insensate.
How can we rid ourselves of this foul leech
That drains the very life blood from our heart?
Push back that which it seems we cannot reach,
And cause the pain and sorrow to depart?
If we would bathe ourselves in tranquil light,
We must cast off the shadows of the night.

Stephen Logan
Age 14

St Paul's College
Raheny
Dublin

Ní Maith Liom Troid

Daoine dána ag troid,
Daoine maithe ag súgradh
Daoine le gunnaí nach bhfuil ag obair.
Daoine le gunnaí atá ag obair.
Tine ar an mbóthar.
Tine ar an rothar.
Tine ar an gcarr.
Tine ar mo theach.
Tine ar an scoil.
Tine ar mo leaba.
Tine ar mo leabhar.

Seán Ó Riain
Age 7

Scoil Bhríde
Ranelagh
Dublin

Things Remind Me

Looking out the window,
Hear the birds sing, leaves rustling,
Horses clopping, sheep bleating,
Remind me of peace.
Fire, bombs, breaking glass
Remind me of war.
I like to listen to waterfalls
Instead of bombs and guns.
I like to look at the sky and the moon
Instead of fire from the war.
O God, please make peace come back.

Sorcha Nic Oibcinn
Age 8

Scoil Bhríde
Ranelagh
Dublin

A New Future

Peace is a word
Quiet, small, yet so strong,
But in each of our hearts
It is where it belongs.

Trying to find it
Is hard sometimes,
Overpowered by greed,
War and arms.

But if we look deep,
Deep in our hearts,
Peace will find a way
To help make a start.

A start to a new future
Of love in mankind,
Where we can all live peacefully
Till the end of our time.

Rebekah Lavelle
Age 11

Holy Cross School
Dublin

The Cease-fire

The Cease-fire, what difference did it make?
It didn't make a difference to me.
The fighting between Catholics and Protestants,
It didn't harm me.
The bombing, the shooting, what did it do?
They harmed families and kids too.
What was the point of the Cease-fire?
It didn't stay for long, it didn't do much good,
But now I wish it would.
Now that I am old enough to understand
I wish the Cease-fire was back again,
So we would not have to live in fear or pain.

Maria Gribbon
Age 15

St Genevieve's High School
Belfast

Is Cuimhin Liom . . .

Is cuimhin liom an radharc . . .

Páistí óga ag súgradh i gcomhluadar a chéile,
A ngutha géara ag líonadh na sráideanna.
Ní thugann siad aird ar aon rud ach
A dtimpeallachta beaga sábháilte - Ógánaigh gan úrchóid.

Agus an bheirt bhan ina seasamh ar an gcúinne,
Ag ráfla go gealgháireach;
Páistí óga i láimh amháin agus málaí siopadóireachta
Sa láimh eile acu.

Os comhair an tí tábhairne,
Scata seanfhear saoithiúil ag déanamh goradh gréine
Ar binse, ina suí go compórdach
Caitheann siad píopaí agus pléann siad an aimsir,
"Tá a stoirm ag éirí," a deir siad.

Lá amháin, phléasc buama . . .

Anois, tá na sráideanna tréigthe, go brónach.
Níl na páistí ag súgradh - tá eagla orthu
Tá na máthaireacha ag caoineadh - tá fearg orthu
Tá na seanfhir ina suí gan focal - tá brón orthu.

Deirtear go bhfuil muintir na hÉireann scriosta
Mar d'fhulaing siad an tragóid leis na blianta anuas.
Deirtear go mbeidh an bua ag an galar sin: éadóchas,
Ach ní chreidim é.

Ná géilligí leo - tá dóchas fós againn in ár gcroíthe
Agus síocháin againn in Éirinn arís
Táim cinnte de.

Vanessa Whyte
Age 17

Wesley College
Dublin

The Song Of The Soldier

The light of the dawn that my sight sings
Is equal to the pain that the night brings.

Empty, I move my hollow husk,
The sky is aflame with the coming of dusk.

And the sound of bombs has died away,
Peace floats down to the world today.

But peace descends to me alone,
For the world has died, I'm on my own.

Seán Down
Age 17

Rathfarnham
Dublin

Give Us Back Our Peace

What is it like to grow up in war?
The fear, the sadness, the frustration, the pointlessness,
The deaths, the killings, the violence and never-ending
carnage,
Is this how we want to bring up our children?
You want it to stop, the days of violence and terror to end,
You cry out for peace, but it's always out of reach.

Why does the war never end?
Why don't people stop the violence and hatred?
If we all work together,
We CAN make a difference.
Does it always have to be like this?
Have we not all had enough?

When peace came to Ulster,
The end of the fear and violence,
We all had so much hope for the future,
Our children to have the chance to grow up in safety,
No need to fear or worry
About the next killing or bombing or show of violence.

Then, one day, in one terrible blow,
In one earth-shattering explosion,
All our hopes of peace were dashed,
And again the peace was lost in Ulster.
In just one terrible day
The violence was back again.

In a matter of seconds
The peace was shattered,
And for the second time
The troubles were back in Ulster.
Yet despite the violence and death,
There will always be hope in Ulster.

I close my eyes and think
Of the day when peace will return,
Of the day when I can feel safe again
In Ulster,
Of the day
When peace will come.

When will the politicians stop arguing
And stop the endless violence,
Give us back our security,
Give us back what I took for granted,
Give us back what we want and need,
Give us back our peace!

Richard McNeill
Age 12

school unknown.

I Want It To Stop

It's a terrible world outside there,
There's someone dying, some place, somewhere.
I want it to stop, I really do.
If I can help, so can you.
We can be a team with a mighty dream,
Or we can be apart, like a body with no heart.
I'd like peace, I really would,
You can help, I know you could.

Gavin Toman
Age 11

St Teresa's Primary School
Glen Road
Belfast

One Day

One day I hope to see the beautiful Dove
Of Peace fly across our sacred land.

One day I hope to see a man without a
Weapon in his hand.

One day I hope to see children playing
In peace with no fear.

One day I hope to see a child's eye
Without a tear.

One day I hope to see a young baby who
Has a fulfilling life ahead.

One day I hope to see a day without
Victims of the troubles lying dead.

One day I hope to see my children
Playing with me or my wife.

One day I hope to see our beautiful
Island with a new lease of life.

Joseph Allsopp
Age 14

St Patrick's
Bearnageeha
Belfast

Thoughts On Peace

Peace is Love.
Peace is Joy.
Peace is Silence and Quiet.
Peace means
No more fighting and
No more killing.

Deborah Doherty
Age 6

Mother of Divine Grace Infant School
Dublin

I like to hear on the news
That peace is on the move.
Peace is great,
I love it so.
You should love it too.
I could not go to school
Or go on my bike for a ride
Or go to a football match
If there was a war outside.

Richard Gow
Age 7

Taney National School
Dublin

I don't want people to blow up houses.
I want people to stop shooting other people.

Ryan Tate
Age 7

Sydenham Primary School
Belfast

No more killing.
No more fighting.
We need peace.
No more war.
We need peace -
Lots of peace.
We need love -
Lots of love.
Lots of love and peace.

Kelly Spain
Age 7

Mother of Divine Grace Infant School
Dublin

There is peace now.
We have no guns.
The school is not afraid.
There is no fighting anymore.

Amanda Calder
Age 7

Sydenham Primary School
Belfast

This poem, written by Julia Crummey and Cíara Gargan, is a letter to Julia's brother, Paul, who was shot dead at the age of four.

To My Brother, Paul

Although I did not know you,
I still feel your pain.
All the pain you once suffered,
I feel it all again.
My brother, four years old, shot dead,
I'm reliving it again.

This is your sister Julia,
The one you never met.
I wish you lived to tell the tale,
To heal the suffering still felt.
We need another ceasefire to lay
Your soul to rest.
I wish it hadn't happened,
Then we could be friends.

Why don't they come together
And give us all an end
To twenty-five years of violence
That is hurting me and other people too?

The IRA, the UVF should give up their arms,
And give us all a rest.

Julia Crummey, Age 12
and Cíara Gargan, Age 13

St Genevieve's School
Belfast

My Peace Wish

If you had a wish,
What would it be?
A new set of clothes?
A new T.V.?

I wish for peace,
I'm not the only one.
I don't want war,
I want to have fun.

People's doors are closed,
What a sad thing to see.
Even my friend's door is closed,
Number forty-three.

Kelly Millar
Age 10

Star of the Sea Primary School
Belfast

Síocháin agus Cogadh

Scoil Bhríde, Ranelagh, Dublin.

Nuair a chloisim na héin ag canadh is nuair a
fheicim na páistí ag súgradh smaoiním ar shíocháin.
Nuair a chloisim daoine ag caoineadh is nuair a
fheicim daoine gortaithe smaoiním ar chogadh.
Is maith liomsa síocháin níos nó ná cogadh.
Tá daoine dána i dtuaisceart na hÉireann.
Tá daoine ag fáil bháis.
Stop ag cur buamaí.

Clár Nic Adhaimh
Age 8

Tá mé ag iarraidh síocháin.
Níl mé ag iarraidh cogadh.
Is maith liom bláthanna, ní maith liom buamaí.
Ní maith liom a bheith ag feáchaint ar dhaoine ag troid.
Is maith liom a bheith ag éisteacht leis na héin.
Ní maith liom a bheith ag éisteacht le daoine ag caoineadh.

Sorcha Nic Oibcinn
Age 8

Smile?

"Smile and look innocent,"
said my mother,
as we approached the crenellated checkpoint.

Why?
I am innocent.
I haven't killed anyone
or planted any bombs.

Why?
Why should I smile?
The grudges will always be borne,
the graffiti covered walls will always stand,
the flags and colours will always fly
and the divisions always remain.

The hard headed soldier grips his weapon
and gives us an undulating gesture,
and as we creep through the jail-like checkpoint,
my mind reflects over past tragedies.

And as we enter the drab, blank streets of Newry
I wonder how folk carry on, void of concern,
when all around them are silent reminders of hell.

Nicola Hanrahan
Age 15

Sutton Park School
Dublin

63

Helicopter Blues

Ain't no peace, just ain't no war
Ain't no peace, just ain't no war
Cause the helicopters buzz outside my windows like before.

They say there's no more fighting, no one more'll die
Then I hear the 'copters rolling thunder in the sky
Ain't no peace, just ain't no war
If everyone's so peaceful then what them 'copters up there for?

When I see ancient history, it starts to get me down
Slogans scrawled on peace walls on the other side of town
Ain't no peace, just ain't no war
Ain't enough divisions so they've gone out and built some more.

None of the politicians know which way to go
All they make are helicopter noises on my radio
Ain't no peace, just ain't no war
One side breaks the window while the other tries to bolt the door.

Freedom fightin' gangsters don't want to see no change
Want to keep my city streets just like a firing range
Ain't no peace, just there ain't no war
If everyone's so peaceful why do they want their shotguns anymore?

Jumpin' on the bandwagon, tryin' to keep us high
Spend money on the television tryin' to close our eyes
Ain't no peace, there just ain't no war
Wonderin' why the open wounds in our memories keep us sore.

Don't ask them reasons, don't try to find out why
But I'll be hearing helicopters until the day I die
Ain't no peace, sure there ain't no war
Anyone with any wit would want to keep their head down on the floor.

Ain't no peace, just ain't no war
Ain't no peace, just ain't no war
Cause still them helicopters buzz outside my windows like before.

Christoper Middleton
Age 16

Methodist College
Belfast

Man's Mask

Slowly he crept up the hill, swinging nervous glances,
Never breaking stride, reached the top, stopped,
Rearing his ugly misshapen body. Mammoth head
twisting,
Peering over the valley beneath, eyes dark, unfathomable,
He saw dark birds arc gracefully into the air,
Turn and zoom over a field of poppies.
A fox appeared, camouflaged by the forest,
Raced out into the open, to flank a retreating rabbit,
Face impassive, unemotional, unreadable he
Rolled down into the field, his giant impossible feet
Tearing the earth from under him, ripping, crushing,
Obliterating.
Suddenly a similarly clad monster appeared from the forest,
Course unaltered and with casual ease,
He swung his long snout toward his mirrored image.
In a brief but explosive exchange of views
His twin was rent asunder,
Showering badly broken bits of steel.
The tank drove on unconcerned.

Scott Tattersall
Age 16

Sutton Park School
Dublin

Death Of The Innocents

Lounging in the soft, cushioned chair,

catching the long drone of sound,

as the vision flickered and continued

as toy cars were sent rolling on the velvety

carpet to their doom.

Childish screams of delight as the cars smashed,

crashed together,

Cracking,

Screaming,

Screeching,

Piercing sounds of death.

Then silence except for the long drone . . .

the cars lay still on the glistening carpet.

Michael McGuinness
Age 17

Sutton Park School
Dublin

Peace is . . .

St Luke's Primary School, Twinbrook, Belfast.

Peace is . . .
no bombs,
and living in harmony.
No fighting and killing,
no chapels being burnt,
and no animals being killed.
No buildings being destroyed,
understanding people's feelings.
Respecting people's opinions.
We all want peace in our land.
Peace in Belfast means so much to me.

Ciara Dodds
Age 9

Peace is a sunny day,
All quiet and calm,
With everyone enjoying themselves
In the nice warm sun.
Peace is a very long book.
No bombs, no killing,
This is good.
Peace in Belfast is a lovely day.
You can send your children to school
Without worrying.
Peace is living in harmony.
I love peace.

Daniel Gourley
Age 9

Peace is where there is no bombing
or no fighting. Peace is
a nice sunny day.
Peace is a very calm and a quiet day
in Belfast.
Sometimes I walk down to the shop
and I see the police
with no guns.
That's good, because sometimes
I think I am going to get shot.

Daniel Kinnaird
Age 9

Peace is living in harmony,
Happily with no killing.
Peace is not being hurt
Or being shot while watching T.V.
Peace is guns and knives
Being locked away forever.
Peace is policemen
Protecting people's property
And the robberies stopping.
Peace is a sunny day,
With no policemen around.
Peace is what everyone wants,
And for once you don't have to buy it.
Peace is the bad groups of people
Stopping fighting and killing.
Peace to me would be really nice,
And I hope one day Ireland has it.

David Finnegan
Age 9

A Plea For Peace

"Stop the war,"
The people say.
"Bring back our peace,"
They kneel and pray.

The guns and bombs
Will sound no more
When peace comes knocking
On their door.

We want our peace,
We want it now,
No more fighting,
Stop this row.

For twenty-five years
They lived in fear,
The bullies refusing to hear
Their plea for peace.

Laura Browne
Age 9

St Brigid's National School
Glasnevin
Dublin

Battlefields

They charge past their fallen comrades
And they do not weep or mourn for them,
For they know that they themselves
Are simply walking corpses.

The battle is over, there were no winners,
Only losers.
Bodies lay strewn across hedges and ditches.
There was no glory,
Only death.

Daniel Sinnott
Age 12

Sandford National School
Dublin

Everytime . . .

Policemen or security men
check my mum's handbag
in the shopping centre
when it is not peace.

Every time I go there
to get something
I see them
standing beside the door.

And people making noises
and you can't get peace there.

Children make a noise
and babies cry
and you can't get peace.

Every time I go there
I hear lots of noise,
babies crying and children shouting.

Ashleigh Watson
Age 6

Sydenham Primary School
Belfast

I Wonder

I wonder when I go to bed
will I wake in one piece,
or like the man next door,
who went to bed and
woke no more.

I wonder is it safe to walk
to school or not.
I wonder will there ever be peace.

Maeve Mateer
Age 10

St Oliver Plunkett National School
Malahide
Co. Dublin

It's Not Fair

It's not fair that people get killed
Just because they are Catholic.
Getting stabbed or shot with a gun,
It must be awful for those who died
And did nothing wrong.

Before peace there was this bomb
That killed a few people.
It's awful for their family.
It is the I.R.A. which planted the bomb,
They can't agree to anything.

When the ceasefire came everyone was full of joy,
It has come to bring peace to Britain
And give me joy. Now,
No horrible wars or bombing attacks,
People have forgot the past.

Just before Christmas Bill Clinton came,
People started laughing and played games.
We tried to show him how peaceful
Our country was, but now he's gone,
We wish he had stayed.

Ashleen Isaac
Age 10

St Luke's Primary School
Twinbrook
Belfast

Little Boy!

So the tall dark tower,
Made of deathforce and power,
Looks down on the frightened face
Of a boy marching in pace,
To the drums of sadness and sorrow.

Why do they always fight,
All day and all night,
Thinking they're brave,
Taking people to the grave,
Saying, "I don't care that I killed you."

We all want peace and joy,
But instead they take your oldest boy.
After they say goodbye
The mother goes off to cry,
As she sees her only son
Is walking the path of the gun.

Alice O'Toole
Age 10

St Matthew's National School
Sandymount
Dublin

Peace To Me

Peace to me
is watching the birds
glide through the sky,
or watching a graceful swan,
drifting on the still water.
Peace to me
is seeing the snow
floating through the frosty air,
or gazing up
into the starlit night sky.
Peace to me
is walking through a forest
of tranquility,
listening to the soothing sounds
of nature.
That would be peace to me.

Dara Geraghty
Age 12

St Matthew's National School
Sandymount
Dublin

Seasons Of Peace

Gazing up at the clouds,
trees swaying in a sudden gust of wind,
swallows dancing in the warm breeze.

Lying embedded in the crystal clear snow,
grey snow clouds roll across the winter sky,
abstract shapes carved into the wintry carpet.

Watching the cherry blossom slowly mature,
lying on the green, dew stung grass,
patiently studying the new born tree buds.

Kicking the dry multi-coloured Autumn leaves,
just plucked from their high perch on the tree
by a passing gust of wind, gently gliding
to settle in their nest on the forest floor.

Mathieu de Courcy
Age 12

St. Mathew's National School
Sandymount
Dublin

Peace To The World

Peace to the world,
That is our dream.
Peace to the world,
O let it be real.
Peace to the world,
That is our wish.
So stop all the fighting
And stop all the bombs
And let all the people
Live together in peace.

Néill Cleary
Age 8

Hedgestown National School
Lusk
Co. Dublin

Views Of Peace

To walk the run of Dunluce
As it slowly slumps into the sea;
Time
Sees all things fall.

To watch a kestrel hover
Above the Giant's Causeway;
Unmoving
In the whispering winds.

To cross Carrick-a-Rede rope-bridge
Leading to a lonely island.
Crossing
To a place of peace.

To climb Knocklayd,
Looking upon Antrim, Rathlin, Scotland,
Seeing
Everything so clearly now.

To stand back and see these sights
As one people
Enables us
To see views of peace.

Andrew Quin
Age 17

St Andrew's College
Blackrock
Co. Dublin

Síocháin agus Cogadh

Scoil Bhríde, Ranelagh, Dublin

Tá síocháin go maith.
Níl cogadh go maith.
Tá na daoine gortaithe go dona.
Tá fuil gach áit.
Tá gunnaí agus buamaí.
Ní maith liom cogadh, is maith liom síocháin.
Tá na buamaí ag gortú na daoine.
Tá na gunnaí ag gortú na daoine.
Tá na daoine i ndáinséar.
Tá daoine ag troid i gcoinne a chéile.

Cal Ó Catháin
Age 8

Na daoine atá ag buamaí!
Stop é anois
Stop an troid daoine dána.
Tá daoine i ndáinséar anois!
Tá Síocháin go maith
Tá Cogadh go dona,
Ordóga in airde do Shíocháin
Ordóga thíos don Chogadh
Na daoine atá ag gáire
Thug siad Síocháin dom.
Thug gunnaí Cogadh dom.
Tá daoine ag iarraidh Síocháin
Tá daoine ag iarraidh Cogadh
Tá mise ag iarraidh Síocháin,
An bhfuil tusa?

Úna Ní Bhrádaigh
Age 8

Where Are My Friends Now

Where are my friends now?
Why have they all left me?
It's not as if I'm dangerous,
My condition's not contagious.

My promiscuous days have long since passed away
All this time, feels like a sentence for a crime
I break down every day.

Where is my family now?
Why can't they protect me
My condition's not contagious
It's not as if I'm dangerous . . .

Draiochta Lundberg
Age 16

Newpark Comprehensive School
Blackrock
Co. Dublin

Peace?

One night I had a dream -
I dreamed I was in a peaceful Belfast.
I was not afraid of terror striking
Because I felt like nothing could harm me,
As long as I was protected by this wall of peace.
Our country's people had quietly united and
Settled down as one, as a bird settles in a nest.
But I was only dreaming.
Surely this dream would never come true.
Still all our people want this life,
Apart from the evil few.
Why do they continue their evil ways
That we are all too used to?
Some day my dreams could be reality,
But I really don't know when.
If only this evil cycle of violence
Would finally come to an end
My dream could come true,
But what I ask is "when"?

David Armstrong
Age 14

Methodist College
Belfast

Ireland

Walking down a lonely street,
Seeing writing on the walls,
"Free the P.O.W.s", "Clegg out", "all out",
What will be next?

Walking down a lonely street,
Frightened of what will happen,
Thinking what if this? What if that?
Or seeing somebody getting beaten up.

Sitting in a lonely house,
Watching reports on the T.V.
"Man shot dead", "Family bombed",
Wondering who's going to be next.

Sitting in a lonely house,
Wondering if you can walk out the door
Knowing that you're not going to die.

We want peace to last,
Not wars and bombs,
We want peace for evermore.

Danielle Lynch
Age 13

St Genevieve's High School
Belfast

Why?

Half truth, half legend,
Half real, half imagined,
Half reluctant, half willing,
Half knowing, half certain.

These are the reasons I do what I do.
People get hurt, a means to an end.
Some die. So why
do I do these things that I do?
I'm sure, so sure. I'm sure, are you?

Declan Finnegan
Age 16

Coláiste Éanna CBS
Ballyroan
Dublin

Who Can Tell The Difference?

Two children going to school,
Same clothes, same shoes,
One is Catholic, one is Protestant.
Who can tell the difference?
No one can.

Two parents going to work,
Same clothes, same shoes,
One is Catholic, one is Protestant.
Who can tell the difference?
No one can.

Two teachers in the staffroom,
Same clothes, same shoes,
One is Catholic, one is Protestant.
Who can tell the difference?
No one can.

Two people trying to make Peace,
Same clothes, same shoes,
One is Catholic, one is Protestant.
Who can help them?
We can!

Ian Horsfield
Age 11

Rathmichael National School
Shankill
Co. Dublin

My Dream

Once there was a ..
I'm not sure,
But it was a something,
I'm sure of it.
What could it be?
I'm sure that I remember it,
Could I be sure that I'm remembering it?
Now I'm sure it began with P, it was very small.
I'm sure of it.
It's not here now,
What could it be?
Now I'm remembering,
It's coming, it's coming,
Oh, it's an E, but now I have a P and an E.
Maybe if I think a little harder
It will come to me.
Aah, now I know,
It was PEACE, but it was very small.
Now why was I thinking about Peace?
Aah, a Peace of cake,
No that's not it.
Peace, let me see what that means.
Oh, it means no fighting and bombing
And innocent people getting killed.
Oh I wish we had PEACE.
How wonderful that would be
For all the people, all of the time,
People living in harmony and safety
Together.

Richard Lawler
Age 13

St Joseph's School for Visually Impaired Boys
Drumcondra
Dublin

The Belfast Bomb

The bang from the bomb boomed around the town,
The people froze in silence, fright and horror.
The screaming of sirens and the shouts of curious people
Echoed in the air.
The shop, flattened like a sandcastle, burying the people within.
The tricolours and the Union Jacks fluttered along the walls.

Peter Wall
Age 13

Sutton Park School
Dublin

Peace On Earth

Peace on earth
And heavenly mild
Has come to beauty
By each little child.
The flowers are blooming,
The birds sing a song,
They know Jesus loves them
All day long.

When Spring comes
Let's all wake up!
Let's all take a cup of Spring,
Of the new fresh breath of Spring.
Now we all know that
It's not all for us,
The creatures of earth
Need to breathe.

Catherine Collins
Age 6

Holy Cross National School
Dublin

Remembrance

As I looked out of my bedroom window
Onto the surrounding hills
They loomed black, enclosing,
Beyond the blacker waters of the loch.
I was young, but not so young
That I could not remember those other
Hills, that rose from that other world,
Not forgotten, but misplaced, unthought of.

Here lies a valley of ashes, of broken dreams,
Where the troublesome times of love and hate
Are entwined with one another like snakes,
Seeking to overcome each other, they retreat
Retiring to regain their strength,
Only to meet once more, twenty-five years later.
The hills grow blacker, unrecognisable now.

I think it will be winter when I die,
For I would not want to die in spring.
A simple unconscious dignity we can never hope
To accomplish will see me to my grave,
And with me will die the now grey heather of those
Murky hills that blossomed yellow, when I was young.

Emily Garvey
Age 16

Sutton Park School
Dublin

War

War is a horrible thing,
Just death and bombs and blood,
There's children suffering everywhere
Because of war in the world.

I cannot understand
Why people want to fight.
There is a better future
If we all do what's right.

There is no fun in fighting.
I hope you all agree
That peace should be restored
In this world, for you, and for me.

Violence doesn't solve a thing,
The only thing it does
Is bring misery and pain
To people who are loved.

I wish the fighting would stop
And then the world could be
A safer place to live and play
For children, like you, and me.

Aisling McGrath
Age 10

St Brigid's National School
Glasnevin
Dublin

Blood Sports

The hunter stands, stares through the smoke of his breath.
His stare freezes with the smallest movement.
Then he moves like a shadow, on and in,
His breath thickens, his heart-beat pulsating, his energy pumps . . .
A shot . . like a single hollow beat of a drum, that echoes,
Spreading out and up.
Then . . nothing. He walks further on into the darkness,
Whispering to himself, the next time his step will be lighter.

Rachael Mullock
Age 16

Sutton Park School
Dublin

91

The White Ribbon Stands For Peace

The white ribbon stands for peace,
not war.
Peace is good, of course,
war is bad.
Peace is when you see
the rustling leaves dropping to sea.
War is bombing, guns and all,
it's not the ribbon at all, at all.
Watching waves is peace,
bombing is war.
That's why peace is best
and war is not.
Help God, not the devil.
God wants peace, so please help.

Rachael Ryan
Age 7

Scoil Bhríde
Ranelagh
Dublin

Peace . . . ?

I'm sick of all the fighting,
I'm sick of all the guns,
I'm sick of all the dying,
An endless war that's never won.

Waking up in the morning,
A new day begins,
"Will we have peace today?"
But the fighting always wins.

Will there be an end to this?
Will the fighting ever cease?
A new day and a new beginning,
Maybe today we will have peace.

Amy Colgan
Age 10

Taney National School
Dublin

I Wish I Was A Peaceful Dove

I wish I was a peaceful dove,
Flying to share my love,
To care for everyone and
To share with everyone.

Hoping there'll be peace,
Praying there'll be peace,
Wishing there'll be peace
Around the world.

Fiona Smith
Age 11

Taney National School
Dublin

Licence To Kill?

Let there be peace in our nation,
Let there be peace in our land,
Let there be joy in our hearts,
Let there be love.

Why should we die for our freedom?
Why should we kill for revenge?
Let there be peace in our hearts,
Let there be love.

Why do we kill one another?
What does it give us but pain?
Why can't we stop, pause and linger?
Why can't we stop pointing the finger?
Why can't we stop allotting blame?
Why can't we all get together
And light the eternal flame?

Let there be peace in our nation,
Let there be peace in our land,
Let there be joy in our hearts,
Let there be love.

Hope the talks still continue,
The truce still prevails.
Let there be peace in our nation,
Let there be love.

Maria Carroll
Age 13

Pobal Scoil Neasáin
Baldoyle
Dublin

Interrogating God

(Aftermath of Dunblane)

How did you let such evil run free?
I'm sorry God, but I really don't see
Why such little, happy minds
Should be attacked and destroyed,
Leaving so many hearts punctured and void.
I'm sorry God, really and truly I am
But I'm finding it hard to keep myself calm
When I think you could have protected
Those tiny, innocent lives
From that evil man and his satanic mind.

Or are you more disgusted
Than anyone else
That the creatures you created
Could get any worse?

Elaine Geary
Age 16

Loreto College
Swords
Dublin

The Gift Of Peace

It is shocking, all the things we see
on our television screens,
The murder, the violence, the men,
women and children who scream.
They scream in sheer terror
because they fear
Being murdered, wounded,
or starved to death.
This sad plight can end with
Peace.
Peace is like a calm sea, with a sunny
blue sky hanging overhead.
But when peace is weakened
the sea becomes rough and
the blue sky vanishes, to leave
dark black clouds
hanging in its place.
So what we need in this world
is friendship and peace.
So God, please give us
the Gift of Peace.

Tomás Langan
Age 11

St Joseph's School for Visually Impaired Boys
Drumcondra
Dublin

War And Peace

The little girl's mother went out at night
When the light from the moon was shining bright.
As she was walking through the street
The terrorist flew by her,
Bullets came flying all around.
The next thing he knows
She's lying on the ground.
He ran away and never came back,
The woman's child
Cried out it pain,
Life for her
Will never be the same again.

She wants some peace in Ulster.

Sarah Close
Age 10

Strand Primary School
Strandburn Street
Belfast

Who's To Gain?

There was a time
When peace did not surround me,
But hatred and war.
Lives of the helpless were robbed,
Destroyed and broken,
Hearts and souls diminished and crushed.
But not mine, nor those of my family,
We were blessed, escaping the terror,
The pain and sorrow.
But not by our own strength,
By grace.
One moment in time might have changed me,
Just one second amongst thousands
Might have quenched my soul
Or torn my pleasant world to pieces.
No, I was blessed, spared,
But not so for all.
The second that saved my life
May have taken that of another,
Crushing the hearts of those left behind,
Tearing them apart.
Thousands of lives ruined or gone,
But for what?
For whose gain?

Debbie Walker
Age 14

School unknown

99

Taps: Two

DAY'S DONE
>And so the night begins
>to draw its
>evil shadow
>over insignificant villages;

GONE THE SUN
>From the streets where joyful
>children once played;

FROM THE SEAS
>And from the
>calm blue lakes, and
>skipping running rivers;

FROM THE HILLS
>And from the lush green fields
>and wooded parks;

FROM THE SKY
>As if it had never set foot
>on this once peacful land.

>So is it true to say that :

ALL IS WELL?
>Or that maybe you now can

SAFELY REST?
>Because you are sure now,
>and always, that

GOD IS NIGH.

David Sanders
Age 16

Sutton Park School
Dublin

We Have All The Time In The World

Could I say something to Mc Guinness?
The bubbles of truth float in peace,
The froth of peace covers the black
Liquid of frustration.
All is contained in a delicate, clear glass,
It can be shattered easily if handled wrong.

Could I say something major?
The blood of lives has tarnished
This country.
A new, white cloth of peace
Could soak up the pain,
Peace can overcome heartache,
And our future could rain.

Lucie Corcoran
Age 15

Newpark Comprehensive School
Blackrock
Co. Dublin

Peace

Grade 1 Students, Age 6, Sutton Park School, Dublin

Peace and quiet,
Don't play with fire.
Share, be kind.
No bombing, no killing,
No drugs.
Helping.
No aeroplanes dropping bombs.
No greed.

Having a nice day,
Having a nice time.

If you lose a game
You don't go out crying.

No spoilsports,
No headaches,
No tears.

Peace and quiet,
Don't play with fire.

You give up,
Retreat.
You shouldn't fight anymore.
Peace to pray.
No children screaming.
No people crying.
No violence.
Sitting down.

A white flag.
Being fair.
If the army ain't fighting, that's peace.

We want peace.
We don't want people's windows falling out.

Éist

Ag éirí na maidine,
Ag deireadh an lae,
Éist, Éist bí cúramach!
"Boom" in oifig an phoist.

Tháinig an t-otharcarr
ach ní raibh aon duine beo,
Leanbh ag caoineadh,
Bean ag guí.

Polaiteóirí ag plé, cách ag guí,
Ag guí, ag plé.
Deireadh an lae.
An mbeidh sólás anois?

Ciarán Ó Maoiléidigh
Age 13

Coláiste Mhuire

School Trip

The school bus makes its way north to Donegal,
we know what is coming,
a little journey an hour or two's length
into a so-called no-man's land.

We pass a tall grey menacing tower,
past walls encompassing fresh-faced boys,
with guns ready to serve in a place they do not want to be.

The bus enters the "real" world, chugging up a hill,
and gets caught in a traffic jam.

Normality . . .
Yes, bar the road signs imported from England.
We are in normality all right.

Conor Crowly
Age 17

Sutton Park School
Dublin

16th February 1996

Every letterbox becomes a green bomb.
Every fast moving car a suicide run.
Your best friend or lover could fall
to the scum.

A red fire blast enough to stun -
The children, the horns, planes,
stars, even stopping the flowers as
they grow.

Bureaucracy becoming so slow, until
it matches the heartbeat of your dead
son.

Is that what we could become,
ordinary people under the siege of
knaves and killers, flesh and blood,
a prison in a prism that separates
love from a cause, life pushed through
a gauze, never stopping to pause -
what have we done? What crime
was committed that we may live by
the monarch of a gun?

Brian Lynch
Age 17

Fingal Community College
Swords, Co. Dublin

Let Us Live In Peace

Let us live in peace,
No more fighting or war.
Let us unite at once
To stop the pain and sore.

Will we unite at once?
Will we unite at all?
Will the peace come back
Or will we divide and fall?

Instead of keeping all our sorrow,
Let the bombing stop tomorrow.
Let us bring back peace in our world,
Let us live in peace now!

Michelle Floyd
Age 12

St Genevieve's High School
Belfast

Nightmares

War is fighting,
War is death,
War is loss of family,
Loss of loved ones,
Which leaves the house deserted.

War makes you trapped
In a hostile world,
Where no one cares
About the suffering of others.
War haunts your dreams,
Turning them into nightmares.

Orla Murphy
Age 9

St Brigid's National School
Castleknock
Dublin

Teachtaireacht Ó Leanaí

Phléasc an buama,
Ligeadh scréach san aer,
Cailín beag bídeach
Ag luí gan bogadh ar'n bhféar.

Ní dhearna sí aon rud,
Ní uirthi an locht
Ach phléasc buama mór,
Sa chathair, i dtrácht.

Íobarthach neamhchiontach eile,
Chuaigh urchar tríd a croí
Cén fáth? Sin an cheist
Atá ag séideadh sa ghaoth.

Anois faoi dheireadh,
Tá síocháin againn,
Tá sí ag teastáil
Cabhraigh linn.

Ná bris na geallúintí,
Ná téigh ar ais,
Tá cead againn súgradh
Nach bhfuil sé go deas?

Tá aosánach na hÉireann,
Tar éis é a rá
Tá síocháin uainn
Sin achaine cách.

Emer Ní Ríain
Age 17

Scoil Mhuire
Templeogue
Dublin

The Border

The early morning dew covers the grass like
a smooth blanket,
The early morning sun blasts cheerfully out of
the blue sky.
The birds sing to their hearts' content;
a lovely day for a drive.
We ramble along the quiet but chirpy
country roads,
We are heading "North".
"North", a word so filled with misinterpretation
and terror in this little green land.
Morning to afternoon, the birds stop singing,
the sky darkens, the atmosphere dampens,
the happiness outside is leaking away
like a waterfall.
We approach a giant metal fort, strewn
with barbed wire and barricades.
Above on the beautiful hilltop with abundant
wild flowers and small tight trees, Now
lies an ugly metal military post with
guns and lenses sticking abruptly out
of bullet-proof panes of glass.

Several men with their metallic faces
drained of emotion utter the same
sentence to the many cars
travelling through.
I pity them, armed to the teeth, ready to
fight for the Queen, I feel uncomfortable,
so many guns, so much hatred, so many
bombs, so much bloody killing,
Why?

Mark Campbell
Age 16

Coláiste Éanna CBS
Ballyroan
Dublin

To Belfast From Sarajevo

Dear Friend,

If only you could share my happiness
and I could share your sorrow.
We would dream together as one
to get rid of war and put peace
in its place.

One day you hear good news,
next day you hear of terror and despair.
People on the street don't care
and politicians don't listen.
One explosion there and another one somewhere else.
People are getting killed and ceasefire is
the light at the end of a dark tunnel.

You don't see children laughing
and people smiling anymore,
differences took them away.
They built a high wall between two peoples,
Protestant and Catholic.
I don't see any difference, my friend.
They are just letters placed in different order
to label people.

If you ever fight with someone
because they are different,
stop and think what caused this war
in the first place.

So good luck, my friend,
take care of yourself.
Don't let this war destroy you,
like it destroyed people's families.
I shared your experience in
Sarajevo, my home.

Your friend from far away.

Alma Somun
Age 15

Pobalscoil Neasáin
Baldoyle
Dublin

What Is That Word?

What is that word again?
It seems to have slipped my memory.
Nor one seems to remember it anymore,
It's the opposite of war.
But I know that word well,
Guns, bombs and blood everywhere,
Yes, I know that word.
But what about that other word?
I even seem to remember it at night,
Flashes of green, black and red.
But what is that other word?
No one seems to know.

Meagan McManus
Age 14

Sutton Park School
Dublin

111

A Troubled Sky

Beneath a dark and dull sky
The dreary rain falls upon the destruction,
Violence and anger rock the innocence of the young and old
And blast it into fear and uncertainty.
Death is often the fate of the innocent,
Caught in the blind destruction.

Beneath a dark and dull sky
Another day pushes by,
Another innocent life is claimed by the blindness,
But the death comes almost unnoticed by the T.V. viewer,
Dismissed as "just another shooting".

Beneath a dark and dull sky
Fear and anger lodge in the minds of the people,
The innocent victims of indiscriminate destruction,
Peaceful efforts crumble, making progress impossible,
And so the bombs and shootings go on.

Conor Cafferkey
Age 13

Sutton Park School
Dublin

Peace Is A Flower

Peace is a flower, protect it
And be rewarded by a beautiful blossom.
Neglected, it wilts and dies,
The blossom of war is death.

War wounds more than bodies,
It wounds minds.
It engraves its pictures on souls.
These pictures, horrific reminders of death,
Eat at minds
And eventually devour them.

Children are the future.
Teach war and war will be the future.
Teach peace and peace will be the future.

Sow the seeds of peace
And the blossoms of peace will bloom.

Laura Finlay
Age 12

Sutton Park School
Dublin

When War Turns To Peace

The quiet city of Belfast
Was once a city of peace.
What rose up throughout our country
Has made us turn for help.
Why can't the troubles all stop
And we can live in one big flock?
For the future of the young
And happiness for the old.

Protestants and Catholics are similar,
They're no different when it comes to peace.
Many vote for war, many vote for peace.
Our bitter wounds can be healed,
Our feelings can be sealed.
With happiness, laughter and pride
There's no more hurt inside.

Thomas McCarthy
Age 11

St Luke's Primary School
Twinbrook
Belfast

Peace In Ireland

To have peace in Ireland
Is all I want to have,
To be outdoors
And play what I want,
To have no violence
Or any death.
So put down your weapons
And stop hurting others.

Gerard McCaffrey
Age 10

St Teresa's Primary School
Glen Road
Belfast

World Peace

Dove of Peace, where are you?
When our world was asleep
You were there.
Our world is awake now,
Awake with shooting.
Where are you?
Bombs are dropped,
Only the innocent suffer.
Hospitals are full of people
Scarred and scared for life.
Families killed one by one.
Children dying, some dead,
Others waiting . . waiting . . waiting . .
Waiting for something to happen.
Guns are allowed when they should not be,
Readied, aimed and fired at us.
The ringing in my ears is so loud.
Why?
Where will it all end?
Let us hope, with peace.

Samantha Twamley
Age 9

Dominican Convent Primary School
Dun Loaghaire
Co. Dublin

A Bond Of Love

Peace is like a bond of love
Flowing through our hearts.
Let us all join the bond
That helps us to be friends.
The killers all can stop their clocks
And look around their world,
And think,
Did God make them to destroy it all?
The answer is all around us.
Look at all the flowers,
Look at all the trees,
Look at all the waterfalls
And the tiny streams.

Charlotte Walker
Age 8

St Matthew's National School
Sandymount
Dublin

Think Again

What are you fighting for?
You know, deep inside, that your cause is obsolete.
You know that your goals mean nothing
When compared with the suffering you have caused.
But you are too proud to admit that neither side is right,
And too proud to lay down your arms, not for us,
Not for yourselves, not even for the children.
But rather you carry on killing - senselessly, indiscriminately,
Shattering the lives of so many.
Not only those who you kill or maim with your bombs
And your guns, and their loved ones, left to mourn their loss,
But all of those, who for so long have lived under your
Reign of terror.
All because you're too proud to stop.

What have you accomplished?
Nothing. You have accomplished nothing
But to cause pain, fear and death.
You have drowned our land with the blood of your victims
And the tears of their loved ones.
You have destroyed so very much
And created nothing of any good.
You have torn apart families, communities.
You have corrupted the children,
Filled their innocent minds with thoughts
Of pain, death and anger.
You have taken away their sweet, precious innocence.
You would have them inherit your anger, your pain
And continue your futile "war".
But still you are not satisfied.

Why won't you stop?
It would seem that you are blind to the death
And destruction you are causing.
It would seem that you are deaf to the screams
Of your victims and the lamenting
Of those left behind to pick up the pieces.
You won't stop because you know nothing but violence.
You won't stop because, still, you have not realised
That violence is not the answer.
You won't stop because you fear that, if you stop,
You'll be forced to answer for your hideous crimes.
Forced to look into the eyes of the child,
Whose parents you murdered in cold blood,
And tell him why.
Tell him why you took his parents away
And caused him to shed so many tears from his innocent eyes.

Barry White
Age 14

Pobalscoil Neasáin
Baldoyle
Dublin

Innocence Of A Child

I guess I never realised
How small she was
Until I saw the coffin.
A small brown box
Containing a small, short life.
It should have been marked "fragile".
It was shrouded with flowers
And remembrance cards.
But who is going to remember her
In six months?
Her killers certainly won't.
"Accident Killing" was the headline,
A stray bullet that shouldn't have been fired,
But was,
Straight through her heart,
Straight through the heart of her mother,
Who must live with the memory.
The box is now covered with earth,
It will be forgotten in time,
But who can forget
The Innocence of a Child.

Sorcha Bangham
Age 15

Loreto Abbey
Dalkey
Co. Dublin

Peace Before Spring

Please can I have peace in Ireland.
My Mammy is going to have a new babby.
She is very happy.
I would love peace for my new babby.
The animals are born in spring.
Let there be Peace before Spring.

Sarah Lowndes
Age 7

St Brigid's National School
Castleknock
Dublin